bridges to contemplative living with thomas merton

advent and christmas

edited by jonathan montaldo & robert g. toth
of the merton institute for contemplative living

ave maria press AmP notre dame, indiana

Every effort has been made to give proper acknowledgment to authors and copyright holders of the texts herein. If any omissions or errors have been made, please notify the publisher, who will correct it in future editions. Ave Maria Press gratefully acknowledges the permission of the following publishers for use of excerpts from these books:

An Endless Trace: The Passionate Pursuit of Wisdom in the West by Christopher Bamford. Copyright © 2003. Used by permission of Codhill Press, Inc.

Contemplative Prayer by Thomas Merton, originally published as *The Climate of Monastic Prayer,* copyright © 1969 by Cistercian Publications. Used by permission of Cistercian Publications.

Listening Below the Noise: The Transformative Power of Silence by Anne D. LeClaire. Copyright © 2009 by Anne LeClaire. Used by permission of HarperCollins Publishers.

Love and Living by Thomas Merton, copyright © 1979 by The Trustees of the Merton Legacy Trust. Used by permission of Harcourt Brace Jovanovich, Publishers.

On Human Being: A Spiritual Anthropology by Olivier Clément. Copyright © 2000. Used by permission of New City Press.

The Psalms: An Inclusive Language Version Based on the Grail Translations from the Hebrew. Published through exclusive license agreement by G.I.A. Publications, Inc. Copyright © 1963, 1986 by The Grail (England). Used by permission of G.I.A.

Raids on the Unspeakable by Thomas Merton. Copyright © 1966 by the Abbey of Gethsemani, Inc. Used by permission of New Directions Publishing Corp.

Run to the Mountain: The Journals of Thomas Merton, Volume One, 1939–1941 by Thomas Merton and edited by Patrick Hart. Copyright © 1995 by the Merton Legacy Trust. Used by permission of HarperCollins Publishers.

Seeds of Destruction by Thomas Merton. Copyright © 1964 by the Abbey of Gethsemani. Copyright renewal 1992 by Robert Giroux, James Laughlin, and Tommy O'Callaghan. Used by permission of Farrar, Straus and Giroux, LLC.

Strangers to the City: Reflections on the Beliefs and Values of the Rule of Saint Benedict by Michael Casey, O.C.S.O. Copyright © 2005, Michael Casey. Used by permission of Paraclete Press.

Founded in 1865, Ave Maria Press is a ministry of the Indiana Province of Holy Cross.

www.avemariapress.com

ISBN-10 1-59471-195-X ISBN-13 978-1-59471-195-4

Cover image © Robert Hill Photography

Interior photograph by Thomas Merton. Used by permission of the Merton Legacy Trust and the Thomas Merton Center, Bellarmine University.

Cover and text design by Andy Wagoner.

Printed and bound in the United States of America.

The decision to accept Christ as the revelation of God's plan for the world is, then, an inexorable renunciation of any attempt to live on two levels at once: one a sacred level, the level of the "soul," of "spirituality," of "recollection" and of "goodness"; and the other a material level of work, distractions, legitimate recreation, power politics, and so on, all of it real enough but somehow unrelated to what goes on in church or in my "interior castle." If Christ is the revelation of the whole meaning of humanity, if the meaning of human life is solely and entirely to be found in the fact that I am a child of God, then everything in my life becomes relevant or irrelevant in proportion as it tends to my growth as a member of Christ, as a child of God, and to the extension of Christ in the world of humankind through his Church.

Thomas Merton
"The Good News of the Nativity"
in *Love and Living*, 1979

A Note about Inclusive Language

Thomas Merton wrote at a time before inclusive language was common practice. In light of his inclusive position on so many issues and his references to our essential unity, we hope these texts will be read from an inclusive point of view.

Contents

Editor's Preface

The previous nine volumes of Bridges to Contemplative Living with Thomas Merton provided eight sessions for small-group dialogue. By contrast, *Advent and Christmas* provides five sessions, one for each week of Advent and one for the Christmas feast of God's Incarnation. Within fewer sessions more has been provided: you will find each session of *Advent and Christmas* more substantial: the texts are longer, the appeal to wider experience more substantive.

Bridges was made for you and your group and not you or your group for this dialogue series. Experiment with how you and your conversation partners use this series as a skillful means to nourish your desire to love God and serve your neighbors.

Since each of these five sessions in *Advent and Christmas* are more generous, you might consider having your group pre-read and reflect upon the texts prior to your meeting. Participants can note what words or ideas in the session most resonate with their own experiences. All of the Bridges volumes, but especially this volume for Advent and Christmas, could serve as texts for private spiritual reading to prepare for the graces of this holy season.

May this volume of Bridges enhance your experience of Advent and Christmas and prepare you to receive a "word for your salvation" that will encourage you to live more joyously, more courageously, and with more hope as you love and serve your neighbors as best you can. Come out, come out, wherever you are: "Come, Lord Jesus!"

Jonathan Montaldo

Introduction

What do we mean by contemplative living?

Life is a spiritual journey. Contemplative living is a way of responding to our everyday experiences by consciously attending to our relationships. It deepens our awareness of our connectedness and communion with others, becomes a positive force of change in our lives, and provides meaningful direction to our journey. Ultimately, contemplative living leads us to a sense of well being, profound gratitude, and a clearer understanding of our purpose in life.

Living contemplatively begins with ourselves but leads us in the end to embrace deeply not only our truest self, but God, neighbor, and all of creation. By reflecting on our everyday experiences, we seek the depths of our inner truth. By exploring our beliefs, illusions, attitudes, and assumptions, we find our true self and discover how we relate to the larger community. Contemplative living directs our minds and hearts to the truly important issues of human existence, making us less likely to be captivated by the superficial distractions that so easily occupy our time.

Who was Thomas Merton?

For over sixty years, the thought and writings of Thomas Merton have guided spiritual seekers across the world. His writings offer important insights into four essential relationships—with self, with God, with other people, and with all of creation. While the Christian tradition is the foundation of his perspective, he was open and inclusive in his examination of other religious traditions, recognizing the important contribution of all faith traditions to the history of civilization. He drew from their strengths to enhance the spiritual growth of individuals and communities.

Thomas Merton was born in Prades, France, in 1915. His mother was from the United States and his father from New Zealand. Educated in France, England, and the United States, he received a master's degree in English from Columbia University. In 1938 he was baptized into the Catholic Church. He taught at St. Bonaventure University for a year and then in 1941 entered the Cistercian Order as a monk of the Abbey of Gethsemani in Kentucky. Directed by his Abbot, Dom Frederic Dunne, Merton wrote his autobiography, *The Seven Storey Mountain*, which was published in 1948.

For fifteen years he served as Master of Scholastics and Novices while writing many books and articles on the spiritual life, interreligious understanding, peace, and social justice issues. In December of 1968, he journeyed to Asia to attend a conference of contemplatives near Bangkok, Thailand. While there he was accidentally electrocuted and died at the age of fifty-three.

Interest in Merton has grown steadily since his death. *The Seven Storey Mountain*, which appears on lists of the one hundred most important books of the last century, has been in print ever since its first edition and has sold millions of copies. The volume of printed work by and about him attests to Merton's popularity. His works have been translated into thirty-five languages and new foreign language editions continue to be printed. The International Thomas Merton Society currently has thirty chapters in the United States and fourteen in other countries.

Thomas Merton is distinguished among contemporary spiritual writers by the depth and substance of his thinking. Merton was a scholar who distilled the best thinking of the best theologians, philosophers, and poets throughout the centuries, from both the West and the East, and presented their ideas in the context of the Christian worldview. His remarkable and enduring popularity indicates that his work continues to speak to the minds and hearts of people searching for answers to life's important questions. For many he is a spiritual guide, and for others he offers a place to retreat to in difficult times. His writings take people into deep places within themselves and offer insight into the paradoxes of life. Merton struggled to be contemplative in a world of action, yet he offered no quick fix or "Ten Easy Steps" to a successful spiritual life.

Using Bridges to Contemplative Living with Thomas Merton

Bridges is intended for anyone seeking to live more contemplatively. For some it initiates a spiritual journey, for others it leads to re-examination or recovery of a neglected spiritual life, and for still others it deepens an already vibrant spirituality. Through reflection and dialogue on specific spiritual themes, participants revisit and refresh their perspectives and understanding of life. They explore the strength and balance of the relationships that ultimately determine who they are: relationships with self, God, others, and nature. Through examining these relationships, participants probe their understanding of life's great questions:

"Who am I?"
"Who is God?"
"Why am I here?"
"What am I to do with my life?"

The selected readings move participants in and out of four dimensions of contemplative living—*Awakening* to an ever-deepening awareness of "true-self"; *Contemplation* of a life experienced from a God-centered perspective; *Compassion* in relationships with others; and *Unity* realized in our undeniable and essential interconnectedness with all of creation. This fourfold process of spiritual formation frames much of Merton's thought and writing.

This is not a spiritual formation program in some "otherworldly" sense. Merton insisted that our spiritual life is our everyday lived experience. There is no separation between them. Bridges does not require an academic background in theology, religion, or spirituality, nor does it require the use of any particular spiritual practices or prayers. There are no levels of perfection, goals to attain, or measurements of progress. This is not an academic or scholarly undertaking. Everyone will find a particular way of contemplative living within his or her own circumstances, religious tradition, and spiritual practices.

The Bridges to Contemplative Living with Thomas Merton series is especially designed for small group dialogue. The selected themes of each session are intended to progressively inform and deepen the relationships that form our everyday lives. Each session begins with scripture and ends in prayer. In between there are time and mental space for spiritual reading, reflection, and contemplative dialogue.

What do we mean by contemplative dialogue?

Contemplative dialogue is meant to be non-threatening, a "safe place" for open sharing and discussion. It is not outcome-oriented. It's not even about fully understanding or comprehending what one reads or hears from the other participants. The focus is on *listening* rather than formulating a response to what another is saying. Simply hearing and accepting another's point of view and reflecting on it can inform and enlighten our own perspective in a way that debating or analyzing it cannot. The pace of conversation is slower in contemplative dialogue than in most other conversations. We are challenged to listen more carefully and approach different points of view by looking at the deeper values and issues underlying them.

Eight Principles for Entering into Contemplative Dialogue

1. Keep in mind that Bridges focuses on our "lived experience" and how the session theme connects to everyday life. Keep your comments rooted in your own experience and refrain from remarks that are overly abstract, philosophical, or theoretical.

2. Express your own thoughts knowing that others will listen and reflect upon what you say. It is helpful to use "I" statements like "I believe . . ." or "I am confused by that response." Try framing your remarks with phrases

such as "My assumption is that . . ." or "My experience has been . . ." While others in the group may very well not respond to you verbally, trust that they are hearing you.

3. Pay attention to the assumptions, attitudes, and experiences underlying your initial or surface thoughts on the topic. Ask yourself questions like: "Why am I drawn to this particular part of the reading?" "What makes me feel this way?"

4. Remember to listen first and refrain from thinking about how you might respond to another's comments. Simply listen to and accept his or her thoughts on the subject without trying to challenge, critique, or even respond aloud to them.

5. Trust the group. Observe how the participants' ideas, reflections, common concerns, assumptions, and attitudes come together and form a collective group mind.

6. Reflect before speaking and be concise. Make one point or relate one experience, then stop and allow others to do the same.

7. Expect periods of silence during the dialogue. Learn to be comfortable with the silence and resist the urge to speak just because there is silence.

8. Avoid cross-talking. In time you will adjust to saying something and not receiving a response and to listening without asking a question, challenging, or responding directly. Simply speaking to the theme or idea from your own experience or perspective takes

some practice. Be patient with yourself and the other members of your group and watch for deepening levels of dialogue.

These principles for contemplative dialogue are extracted from the work of the Centre for Contemplative Dialogue. For more complete information visit www.contemplativedialogue.org.

Additional Resources

A leader's guide and introductory DVD for the Bridges series are available from Ave Maria Press.

Online resources available at www.avemariapress.com include:

- Leader's Guide
- Sample pages
- Suggested Retreat Schedule
- Program Evaluation Form
- Links to other books about Thomas Merton
- Interview with Robert Toth of the Merton Institute for Contemplative Living

From the Merton Institute for Contemplative Living:

www.mertoninstitute.org

Merton: A Film Biography (1 hour) provides an excellent overview on Merton's life and spiritual journey.

Soul Searching: The Journey of Thomas Merton is a sixty-seven-minute DVD that goes to the heart of Merton's spiritual journey through the perspective of Merton's friends, Merton scholars, and authorities on the spiritual life.

Contemplation and Action is a periodic newsletter from the Merton Institute with information about new Merton publications, programs, and events. It is free and can be obtained by visiting the institute's website or calling 1-800-886-7275.

The Thomas Merton Spiritual Development Program is a basic introduction to Merton's life and his insights on contemplative spirituality, social justice, and interreligious dialogue. Especially designed for youth, it includes a participant's workbook/journal.

Weekly Merton Reflections: Receive a brief reflection from Merton's works via e-mail each week by registering at www.mertoninstitute.org or by contacting:

The Merton Institute for Contemplative Living
2117 Payne Street
Louisville, KY 40206
1-800-886-7275

First Week of Advent
Hope

Opening Reflection

Psalm 27:7–9, 11, 13–14

O Lord, hear my voice when I call;
have mercy and answer.
Of you my heart has spoken:
"Seek his face."

It is your face, O Lord, that I seek;
hide not your face.
Dismiss not your servant in anger:
you have been my help.

Instruct me, Lord, in your way;
on an even path lead me.

I am sure I shall see the Lord's goodness
in the land of the living.
Hope in him, hold firm and take heart.
Hope in the Lord!

Introduction to the Texts

We cannot serve two masters. We cannot listen equally well to the Good News of the Incarnation and to the clatter of a secular season of pious sentiments and credit cards. We cannot equate a financial quarter of accelerated commercial activity with the Church's Advent call for repentance. Advent disposes us to conversion and single-mindedness. We are called to attend to our deepest needs and hopes: to realize the mitigation of human suffering through daily deeds of compassion for and service to our neighbors.

In his essay "The Good News of the Nativity" Thomas Merton presented Advent as a time for discerning what is most relevant for us individually and communally in this moment of our being alive together in history.

> If Christ is the revelation of the whole meaning of humanity, if the meaning of human life is solely and entirely to be found in the fact that I am a child of God, then everything in my life becomes relevant or irrelevant in proportion as it tends to my growth as a member of Christ as a child of God, and to the extension of Christ in the world of humankind through his Church.

Advent then is a time for judging the choices we make in how we are living out our lives. Advent is a ritual moment for confronting discomforting truths. It catches us in the act of living unconnected from the Gospel, as if we were being photographed cutting into a steak at a restaurant's window while another human being on the other side of the pane stands mesmerized by the size of the meat on our forks. Advent overturns our complacencies to realize the exceedingly narrow but true way of Christian discipleship. If we receive the good news of Christmas, let us attempt to accept Jesus' hard stuff. Throughout Advent we need to heed the warning of Olivier Clément:

> Every one who relinquishes the security of a sleepwalking existence is sooner or later

mortally wounded by the world's suffering. But because God became man and took this suffering on himself, the way of vulnerability and death becomes for us resurrection.

—*On Human Being*, p. 58

Merton's Voice

From *Raids on the Unspeakable*

We live in a time of no room, which is the time of the end. The time when everyone is obsessed with lack of time, lack of space, with saving time, conquering space, projecting into time and space the anguish produced within them by the technological furies of size, volume, quantity, speed, number, price, power, and acceleration.

The primordial blessing, "increase and multiply," has suddenly become a hemorrhage of terror. We are numbered in billions and massed together, marshaled, numbered, marched here and there, taxed, drilled, armed, worked to the point of insensibility, dazed by information, drugged by entertainment, surfeited with everything, nauseated with the human race and with ourselves, nauseated with life.

As the end approaches, there is no room for nature. The cities crowd it off the face of the earth.

As the end approaches, there is no room for quiet. There is no room for solitude. There is no room for thought. There is no room for attention, for the awareness of our state. . . .

In the time of the end there is no longer room for the desire to go on living. The time of the end is the time when men call upon the mountains to fall upon them, because they wish they did not exist.

Why? Because they are part of a proliferation of life that is not fully alive, it is programmed for death. A life that has not been chosen, and can hardly be accepted, has no more room for hope. Yet it must pretend to go on hoping. It is haunted by the demon of emptiness. And out of this unutterable void come the armies, the missiles, the weapons, the bombs, the concentration camps, the race riots, the racist murders, and all the other crimes of mass society.

Is this pessimism? Is this the unforgivable sin of admitting what everybody really feels? Is it pessimism to diagnose cancer as cancer? Or should one simply go on pretending that everything is getting better every day, because the time of the end is also—for some at any rate—the time of great prosperity? ("The Kings of the earth have joined in her idolatry and the traders of the earth have grown rich from her excessive luxury" [Rev 18:3]). (pp. 70–72)

Another Voice

Gerard Thomas Straub, *Falling Silent*

In his book, *No Man Is an Island,* Thomas Merton wrote: "There must be a time of day when the man who makes plans forgets his plans, and acts as if he had no plans at all. There must be a time of day when the man who has to speak falls very silent. And his mind forms no more propositions, and he asks himself: Did they have any meaning? There must be a time when a man of prayer goes to pray as if it were the first time in his life he had ever prayed; when the man of resolutions puts his resolutions aside as if they had all been broken, and he learns a different wisdom: distinguishing the sun from the moon, the stars from the darkness, the sea from the dry land, and the night sky from the shoulder of a hill" (*No Man Is an Island*, 260).

I am at that time of day.

A time to fall silent and be still, a time to look deeply into the essence of my life, the essence of life itself, so much of which makes absolutely no sense. And because it makes no sense, I kept moving, kept doing in order not to be overcome by the apparent meaninglessness of it all.

I am in that time of day when I can sit alone . . . and ponder and pray.

This state of being alone has been forced upon me. I would not have had the courage to choose it myself, though I had within me a faint desire for genuine solitude.

I am at that time of day when I can give the day the time it deserves, the time required to allow something real to happen. I am at that time of day when I can be both silent and attentive . . . attentive to birds flying around my yard, and attentive to the flock of thoughts flying around inside of me.

I am at that time of day when I am free, free to find and love myself . . . and God. All the things that have been pulling at me for years, demanding my full attention, such as the endless responsibility of trying to right the injustice of chronic poverty, have suddenly vanished like a poorly constructed building in Haiti toppled by an earthquake.

I am at a *kairos* time of day, a time when I can give myself a chance to let go of everything I know in order to be carried along by the flow of all I do not know, the very flow of the mystery and true reality of life. Speaking about prayer and the essence of what we truly need, Thomas Merton said, "We don't have to rush after it. It is there all the time, and if we give it time, it will make itself known to us."

I am going to give it time. I am going to enter the invisible chamber of my soul where I will try to shut out all cares, worries, distractions, idle thoughts . . . shut out all but God as I wait for God. Oddly enough, say all the saints and mystics, God is already there. It is I who am missing, hidden in the rubble of my own life, buried under the weight of my countless faults, failures, mistakes, and illusions. Now is the time to cast off the burden of the past with all its missteps, concern for the future with all its sudden uncertainty and seek to see the face of God in this present moment, in this *kairos* time of day.

I pray that the emptiness and darkness does not scare me, does not prompt me to seek the false light of the world and all its empty promises and illusions. My past experience has taught me that whenever the light of God truly penetrates my inner being, I am able to see clearly how far I am from God, how great the contrast is between who and what God is and who and what I am. This is a time for renewal, a time for rejuvenation, a time to enter the fullness of life.

We live in dark times, in an age of deep despair. Without an inner sense of depth and freedom we easily become oppressed by the darkness and despair, victims of our circumstances. With God, we can see and move beyond our limitations. God created us for growth, for an ever-expanding realization of the divinity within us. In God, there is true freedom. Outside of God, there is only bondage.

For me, seeing so much suffering in the massive slums of the world forced me to forget myself, my own limitations, and hear the silent voice of God calling me to respond, not only to the shameful injustice, but also to God's endless mercy and love. In seeing so many starving kids with bloated bellies and the overwhelming need of the poor, I became less concerned with my own subjective needs and harmful compulsions, and more aware of the self-emptying love of Christ which I needed to imitate to the best of my ability. But the noise of life sometimes distracted me and rendered me deaf to God and capable of only hearing my own confused and rambling voice.

Without the stillness and silence of solitude, we easily slip back into the mediocrity of a comfortable Christianity which is no match for the gun-toting, hopeless nihilism of postmodern life where everything is reduced to a commodity for sale, where unbridled greed has caused a catastrophic global economic recession, where materialism without qualification and sex without love are affirmed and championed, where mainstream corporations distribute pornography without shame or reproach, where dialogue has given way to vitriolic hate speech, where conflicts are settled by violence, where barbarous acts of terrorism threaten all, where blind religious fundamentalism passes for true faith, where drug addiction and alcoholism are rampant, where thousands of kids die every day from hunger, and where selfishness and individualism have created prisons of poverty and are destroying the earth. In stillness and silence we are able to catch a glimmer of the interconnectivity of all life, to see the sun as our brother and the moon as our sister, to see that all of humanity and all of creation as part of our family.

Even in solitude I am powerless to create (or even merit) the desire of my heart, the desire to see the face of God. It is only by grace that God gives us eyes to see, ears to hear, and a heart to understand. And the lived reality of God's grace and presence leads us, in our own fragility, to greater and greater heights of compassion for others.

Reflect and Dialogue

What images, words, or sentences in these readings most resonate with your experiences? In what ways do they resonate?

In what ways are you choosing to "sleepwalk through your existence"?

Whose suffering this Advent do you wish to console and share as if it were your own?

What does the season of Christmas mean for the youth and young adults in your family?

Closing

Conclude with one of the meditations on pages 57–58 or with a period of quiet reflection.

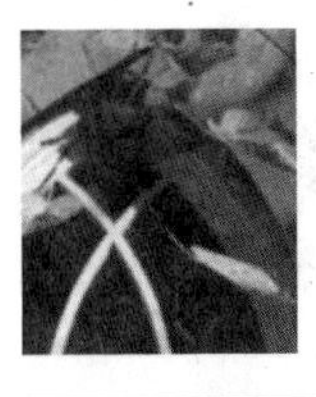

Second Week of Advent
SALVATION

OPENING REFLECTION

PSALM 40:2, 4A, 7, 9

I waited, I waited for the Lord
and he stooped down to me;
he heard my cry.

He put a new song into my mouth;
praise of our God.

You do not ask for sacrifice and offerings,
but an open ear.

In the scroll of the book it stands written
that I should do your will.
My God, I delight in your law
in the depth of my heart.

INTRODUCTION TO THE TEXTS

Thomas Merton arrived at the gates of the Abbey of Gethsemani during Advent, on December 10, 1941. He always remembered this season of his wanting to become a monk, and described it in his journals as a "time of walking on water." He was like Peter leaving the boat and walking toward Jesus whom he trusted to catch him should he fall.

Merton celebrated his first Christmas at Gethsemani realizing that he had found his life's sacred place where he could best listen for the revelation of God's voice to him, telling him that he was loved and that he should return this love by serving his neighbor. Merton transcribed a prayer to his journals during the dark hours of his first Christmas Eve at Gethsemani. He found himself waiting on God in silence and expectancy, realizing that he did not know who God truly was for him, but he was praying in hope that through his silent vigil and attention, he would be graced, beyond his imagination, to hear God's own true voice:

> Lord, it is nearly midnight and I am waiting for you in the darkness and the great silence. I am sorry for all my sins. Do not let me ask any more than to sit in the darkness and light no lights of my own, and be crowded with no crowds of my own thoughts to fill the emptiness of the night in which I await you. . . .
>
> Your brightness is my darkness. I know nothing of you and, by myself, I cannot even imagine how to go about knowing you. If I imagine you, I am mistaken. If I understand you, I am deluded. If I am conscious and certain I know you, I am crazy. The darkness is enough.
>
> —*Run to the Mountain*, Journals Volume 1: 310

Merton's Voice

From *Contemplative Prayer*

Contemplative prayer is, in a way, simply the preference for the desert, for emptiness, for poverty. One has begun to know the meaning of contemplation when one intuitively and spontaneously seeks the dark and unknown path of aridity in preference to every other way. The contemplative is one who would rather not know than know. Rather not enjoy than enjoy. Rather not have *proof* that God loves him. He accepts the love of God on faith, in defiance of all apparent evidence. This is the necessary condition, and a very paradoxical condition, for the mystical experience of the reality of God's presence and of his love for us. Only when we are able to "let go" of everything within us, all desire to see, to know, to taste, and to experience the presence of God, do we truly become able to experience that presence with the overwhelming conviction and reality that revolutionize our entire inner life. . . .

Contemplation is essentially a listening in silence, an expectancy. And yet, in a certain sense, we truly begin to hear God when we have ceased to listen. What is the explanation of this paradox? Perhaps only that *there is a higher kind of listening*, which is not an attentiveness to some special wave length, a receptivity to a certain kind of message, but a general emptiness that *waits to realize the fullness of the message of God within its own apparent void* [emphasis added]. In other words, the true contemplative is not the one who prepares his mind for a particular message that he wants or expects to hear, but is one who remains empty because he knows that he can never expect to anticipate the word that will transform his darkness into light. He does not even anticipate a special kind of transformation. He does not demand light instead of darkness. He waits on the Word of God in silence, and when he is "answered," it is not so much by a word that bursts into his silence. It is by his silence itself suddenly, inexplicably revealing itself to him as a word of great power, full of the voice of God. (pp. 89–90)

Another Voice

Anne D. LeClaire, *Listening Below the Noise: The Transformative Power of Silence*

Eventually I stopped agonizing over my desire for time apart and what it implied. Hadn't my silent days initially been met with resistance and curiosity, even judgment? And hadn't they proved to be enriching? Hadn't I learned that silence and solitude could strengthen my connection to others? Hadn't it been solitude and silence that taught Thomas Merton to love his brother monks?

So as I had once committed to staying speechless on the first and third Mondays, I now dedicated part of those days to solitary time.

Alone, with my thoughts for company, I befriended my private self, all of me, my weaknesses and my fundamental worthiness. That was the challenge and the reward to alone time. In my garden plot of stillness and solitude, I reflected on matters of critical introspection that the pace and demands of modern life seldom allow time for. What do I believe? How do I want to spend the capital that is the time I am given on earth? What kind of partner am I to my husband? What kind of mother to my children? What is selfishness and what is self-care? What do I fear? What are my prejudices? How can I overcome them? What are my intentions? Like the lone oak tested by storms, I found that solitude was strengthening the roots of my personality and fertilizing the place where wisdom resides. And, like its sister, silence, solitude slowed me down.

I felt as if layers and layers of skin had been sloughed. I was moved to tears by things as simple as the sight of a hawk soaring overhead. Or the kindness of a stranger.

I would be derailed for long minutes, observing things that on an ordinary day I would brush right past. I was enthralled by squirrels leaping between the limbs of the oaks in our backyard, the interplay of baby chickens in the coop by our garage, the intricate beauty of a yellow and black spider on a windowsill.

These things not only pulled my attention but also seemed infinitely worthy of consideration. Like a squatting child engrossed and enchanted by the activity of an anthill, I was mesmerized by life. And watching, I wondered, is there anything in nature that doesn't sit in itself calmly? (pp. 176–177)

Reflect and Dialogue

What images, words, or sentences in these readings most resonate with your experiences? In what ways do they resonate?

How would you explain in your own words and in the context of the above reading Merton's paradox that "We truly begin to hear God when we have ceased to listen"?

Through your daily living, in what ways, through which media, do you sense you hear God's voice?

How have you sought silence and solitude in your life and what has it harvested in you?

Closing

Conclude with one of the meditations on pages 57–58 or with a period of quiet reflection.

Third Week of Advent
Compassion

Opening Reflection

Psalm 85:9–12, 14

I will hear what the Lord God has to say,
a voice that speaks of peace,
peace for his people and his friends
and those who turn to him in their hearts.
His help is near for those who fear him
and his glory will dwell in our land.

Mercy and faithfulness have met;
justice and peace have embraced.
Faithfulness shall spring from the earth
and justice look down from heaven.

Justice shall march before him
and peace shall follow his steps.

Introduction to the Texts

The Church's sacred texts proclaimed during Advent and Christmas educate us in realizing that God has truly come among us in the person of Jesus so that our daily lives are attended by God's presence embodied in those with whom we eat our share of life's banquet, celebrating being alive together, sometimes in joy and often in tears. Heeding Jesus' command that we love one another, we choose to love the world in the company of those with whom we share it every day. To love one another implies a daily struggle against whatever in our complex, double- and triple-minded selves urges us to refrain from participating fully in the life of the world into which we have been born. The contemplative struggles to keep lit the flame of the candle that has been entrusted solely to him or her in order to make the world less dark.

The Son of God became flesh to announce the Good News that the Kingdom of God is within us and that the Holy Spirit has been sent to support our relationships with all beings ("God is love"). Thomas Merton received the Good News of the Incarnation as a word of freedom that unlocked his liberty to participate in the particular history given to him, so that he might—beyond his selfishness—serve his neighbors. "The freedom of the Christian contemplative is not freedom *from* time, but freedom *in* time."

Merton's Voice

From *Seeds of Destruction*

The contemplative life is not, and cannot be, a mere withdrawal, pure negation, a turning of one's back on the world with its sufferings, its crises, its confusions, and its errors. First of all, the attempt itself would be illusory. No man can withdraw completely from the society of his fellow men; and the monastic community is deeply implicated, for better or for worse, in the economic, political, and social structures of the contemporary world. To forget or to ignore this does not absolve the monk from responsibility for participation in events in which his very silence and "not knowing" may constitute a form of complicity. The mere fact of "ignoring" what goes on can become a political decision. . . .

This is not to say that the monk is obliged to partisan commitment, and that a contemplative should take this or that specific political line. On the contrary, the monk should be free of the confusions and falsities of partisan dispute. The last thing in the world I would want is a clerical or monastic movement in politics!

Yet I hold that the contemplative life of the Christian is not a life of abstraction, of secession, in order to concentrate on ideal essences, upon absolutes, upon eternity alone. Christianity cannot reject history. It cannot be a denial of time. Christianity is centered on an historical event that has changed the meaning of history. The freedom of the Christian contemplative is not freedom *from* time, but freedom *in* time. It is the freedom to go out and meet God in the inscrutable mystery of his will here and now, in this precise moment in which he asks man's cooperation in shaping the course of history according to the demands of divine truth, mercy, and fidelity.

The monastic flight from the world into the desert is not a mere refusal to know anything about the world but a total rejection of all standards of judgment which imply attachment to a history of delusion, egoism, and sin. Not of course a vain denial that the monk too is a sinner (this would be an even worse delusion), but a definitive refusal to participate in those activities which have no other fruit than to prolong the reign of untruth, greed, cruelty, and arrogance in the world of men.

The monastic withdrawal from secular time is then not a retreat into an abstract eternity but a leap from the cyclic recurrence of inexorable evil into the eschatological Kingdom of God, in Christ—the kingdom of humility and of forgiveness.

The adversary is not time, not history, but the evil will and the accumulated inheritance of past untruth and past sin. This evil the monk must see. He must even denounce it, if others fail to do so. (pp. xiii–xiv)

Another Voice

Olivier Clément, *On Human Being: A Spiritual Anthropology*

As Christians we know that by participating in history we are not going to turn it into the Kingdom of God. But our horizon is not limited to history; we know that Christ is coming again in glory to raise all the dead and, through them, the flesh of the world and all that history has created. With this hope we have no need of Utopia.

Christians are making ready within history a transformation that will surpass it, the transformation that is already secretly accomplished in Christ. Thus they escape the dilemma of "all or nothing." Nor do they simply accept things as they are, like the hopeless or the well-to-do. They are watchful for every opportunity of promoting freedom, justice, or dignity. Their struggle—an inner struggle to begin with—is neither conservative nor revolutionary, nor even both at once. The conservatism of Christians is not the same as the cynicism and fear felt by those who have too much, who are all the more willing to theorize abut the intractability of history for having themselves benefited from it. Christians cannot stay far from the abandoned and the rebellious. But even while aware of the chances of life, and their tragic consequences in history, we nevertheless know that there are principles, virtually biological laws, by which social life is harmonized with the life of the universe; that the tension between the individual and society is irreducible, and that in politics more than anywhere else "he who would be an angel behaves like a beast"; the makers of paradise have been the tormentors from hell; and the liver of Prometheus is gnawed away by pollution. Humankind needs justice and happiness, but also risk, transcendence, and the profound tragedy of existence. The struggle against "the spirit of heaviness," against stupidity and hatred, is never-ending. Only a hope anchored beyond the world—but already transforming the world through personal beings—can give us the patience to serve life without falling into bitterness or despair.

Christians may not be revolutionary as popular mythology understands the term, but they know that there is a revolutionary force within Christianity, that of Christ the vanquisher of death. This force can alter the make-up of the person. And if this change takes place simultaneously in several people who are in communion, then the world begins to change, and a civilization is founded. (pp. 99–100)

Reflect and Dialogue

What images, words, or sentences in these readings most resonate with your experiences? In what ways do they resonate?

How has your Christian experience of God given you freedom to love and serve the world?

How would you answer your daughter if she asked you where is the hope? What is the use of "watching for every opportunity of promoting freedom, justice, or dignity" in her life?

How are you "cooperating in shaping the course of history according to the demands of the divine truth, mercy, and fidelity"?

Closing

Conclude with one of the meditations on pages 57–58 or with a period of quiet reflection.

Fourth Week of Advent
Tenderness

Opening Reflection

Psalm 148:1–4, 7–13

Alleluia!

Praise the Lord from the heavens,
praise him in the heights.
Praise him, all his angels,
praise him, all his hosts.

Praise him, sun and moon,
praise him, shining stars.
Praise him, highest heavens
and the waters above the heavens.

Praise the Lord from the earth,
sea creatures and all oceans,
fire and hail, snow and mist,
stormy winds that obey his word;

all mountains and hills,
all fruit trees and cedars
beasts, wild and tame,
reptiles and birds on the wing;

All earth's kings and peoples,
earth's princes and rulers;
young men and maidens,
old men together with children.

> Let them praise the name of the Lord
> for he alone is exalted.
> The splendor of his name
> reaches beyond heaven and earth.

Introduction to the Texts

Once he initially realized her presence in his life during a visit to Cuba, Thomas Merton's devotion to Mary, the mother of his salvation and of his vocation to the priesthood, never wavered. He realized Mary's role in his life as the sacramental energy of God's mercy toward him. On the universal level in Merton's religious imagination, Mary was the sacrament of God's inclusive tenderness for the world. Merton wrote that "in this narrative of the miraculous virgin birth of the Lord, as recited in the early Church, we have a revelation of the infinite motherly compassion of God for humanity, a revelation which is not only absolutely without error but which, by reason of the special "feminine" cast of its literary expression, tells us something quite unique that we would otherwise never apprehend."

Mary, the mother of Jesus and the mother of Merton's own monastic and priestly vocation, was a continuing presence in his prayers, poetry, and journals. She was the primary agent of God's benevolence toward Merton throughout his life. His written prayers to Mary were always characterized by filial piety. It was she who led him across the waters from England and opened the way for him to "another country" where he could live "in Christ" at the Abbey of Gethsemani:

> And when I thought there was no God and no love and no mercy, you were leading me all the while into the midst of his love and his mercy

> and taking me, without my knowing anything about it, to the house that would hide me in the secret of his face.
>
> —*The Seven Storey Mountain*, p. 130

Hail Mary, full of grace, blessed among women, blessed is the fruit of your womb, Jesus. Holy Mary, Mother of God, pray for us sinners, now and at the hour our death, Amen.

Merton's Voice

From *Love and Living*

The full Christian sense of the person is found in the recovery of our likeness to God, in Christ, by his Spirit. This, in turn, is attained only in that relationship of personal love that is established, in the Church, with all who have heard the same message and responded to it in the one Spirit. It is this grace, this stupendous gift and possibility, this power to be made new, not only individually, but as *Ecclesia*, as "*one new man*," which is announced in the great joy of the Nativity Gospel. It is the theological fact which the Church celebrates in the paschal liturgy and which is extended to all feasts, especially to Christmas, with proper individual aspects.

The details of the Nativity—the way it is related, the incidents that are selected by each evangelist, the theological points that each one emphasizes—all serve to bring home to us this *inner revelation* [emphasis added], which the Church at once announces (in her *kerygma* [her proclaiming the Gospel]) and celebrates (in her liturgy). Matthew, for instance, seeks to show in how many ways that the birth of Christ is the fulfillment of the Old Testament messianic prophecies, and therefore how, in Christ, the whole meaning and aspiration of the Old Testament is completed and made plain. Luke, with a human and compassionate charm, brings out what St. Paul called the goodness of God and his tender love for men (Ti 3:4). Whether or not Luke sat down and dutifully took it all down at the dictation of the Blessed Mother we can hardly know; but the fact remains that there is a feminine aspect in the Nativity recital according to Luke. This tenderness (so well expressed in the *umileny* [Mary as tender mother] icons of the Russian Church) fills out the theological picture of God's mercy to humanity in the Incarnation. Tender maternal love is inseparable from the whole theology of Mary, the Mother of God.

We may argue until doomsday about whether the angel who appeared to Mary came in through the window or through the wall, whether it was midnight or ten in the morning, or, indeed, whether there was an angel at all (was it perhaps just a bright idea?). The fact remains that, in this narrative of the miraculous virgin birth of the Lord, as recited in the early Church, we have a revelation of the infinite motherly compassion of God for men, a revelation which is not only absolutely without error but which, by reason of the special "feminine" cast of its literary expression, tells us something quite unique that we would otherwise never apprehend.

Now it is this unique aspect of the divine mercy, an aspect which is so powerfully suggested by the poetry of Luke but can never be reduced to scientific language, that is precisely what the Christian heart obscurely senses in responding to the Gospel of the Nativity as read and understood by the Church. (pp. 226–228)

Another Voice

Michael Casey, O.C.S.O., *Strangers to the City: Reflections on the Beliefs and Values of the Rule of Saint Benedict*

In the view of Claude Peifer "monasticism grew out of the most devout circles of the second- and third-century Church, the virgins and ascetics, and was strongly marked with the imprint of the spirituality of martyrdom [*RB 1980: The Rule of St. Benedict in Latin and English with Notes*, p. 361]." The workaday spirituality that powered fervent monastic lives was simply personal devotion to the person of Christ. If in the monasteries this *affectus cordis* [heart movement] was more ardent than in the Church in general, it was simply because an existence that was ordinary, obscure, and laborious needed greater interior stimulus if it were not to collapse into a sterile regime of pious inertia.

This love for Christ rose to a crescendo among the Cistercians of the twelfth century, who needed a strong counter-balance to the excess of fear prevailing in religious circles. The first generations of Cistercian monks were all adult recruits who were presumed, generally speaking, to have pursued lives of youthful self-indulgence with sufficient zest to warrant a radical conversion. In the monastery they lived a rugged macho existence with little comfort and a more-than-usual degree of bodily exertion and austerity. To service the interior needs of these tough young males a complementary spirituality developed, which has been described by Jean Leclercq as a "feminine" spirituality.

In the monasteries, personal love for Jesus was supplemented by a devotion to four feminine realities, made easier by the gender of the Latin words: *Anima*,

Sapientia, Ecclesia, Maria. The monk's devotion to an interior life was governed by principles complementary to his masculine exterior life. The life of the soul was seen as running along a complementary track to the life of the body. It was understood as the search for Lady Wisdom or Sophia; devotion to Christ's bride, the Church, care of one's own soul and—beyond these *hypostatizations* [inspired ideas realized as enfleshed]—a deep personal attachment to Mary, not only as the mother of the historical Jesus, but also as a mother, advocate, and patron in one's own spiritual journey.

The Cistercian spirituality of this era was uncompromising in its demand for single-mindedness, expressed externally by a rigorous life that was the opposite of self-indulgence, and internally by an equally exigent pursuit of unblinking self-knowledge. Yet, at the level of personal experience, there is only tenderness, gentleness, and an overriding confidence in the all-accepting mercy of God: a soft spirituality but—be warned!—one that loses all meaning if separated from its hard tegument. Bernard [of Clairvaux] often reminds us that in the house of Bethany there can be no Mary without Martha and Lazarus: the labor of penance and the generosity of service are the indispensable buttresses to the joy of contemplation.

The word that epitomizes this experience-oriented spirituality is *dulcedo*, sweetness. It is unfortunate that the term has become debased through the flowery excesses of pietism. Monastic life presupposes all sorts of external observances and deprivations, but these are secondary. What drives them is an untrammeled interior affectivity that has its focus on the person of Christ, but is necessarily both unconditional and unrestricted in those to whom it reaches out. This is not a grim life in which the monk labors at breaking his egotism as a convict might break rocks. It is more a matter of allowing oneself to fall under the sway of the attractiveness of God that lesser realities lose their charm. At those moments when we let go of alternative satisfactions, God's presence activates the deepest zone of selfhood; something within us flares into life with an unpredictable intensity so that we experience ourselves as drawn to God, lost in God, one with God, divinized. We have tasted and seen for ourselves that the Lord is sweet. (pp. 145–146)

Reflect and Dialogue

What images, words, or sentences in these readings most resonate with your experiences? In what ways do they resonate?

Who is Mary, the mother of Jesus and Mother of the Church, for you?

Do you experience the energy of Mary's action of "fiat" in the Gospel According to Luke? In what ways do you experience it?

How do you understand the religious symbolism that we are all one in a "community of saints"?

Closing

Conclude with one of the meditations on pages 57–58 or with a period of quiet reflection.

Christmas

The Word Made Flesh

Opening Reflection

Psalm 98:1–4

Sing a new song to the Lord
for he has worked wonders.
His right hand and his holy arm
have brought salvation.

The Lord has made known his salvation;
has shown his justice to the nations.
He has remembered his truth and love
for the house of Israel.

All the ends of the earth have seen
the salvation of our God.
Shout to the Lord all the earth,
ring out your joy.

Introduction to the Texts

Saint Bernard of Clairvaux, the twelfth-century Cistercian and Doctor of the Church, imagined that Christ was continually being born in all of us as we journeyed toward maturity in communion with Jesus through the Holy Spirit to the Father. Our Christian destiny, in Saint Bernard's view, is for each person to mature into a particular and original human face, a unique image of God from which each person's inner life "in Christ" could shine through to light the world.

In his Christmas sermon, Merton appropriates the Good News of the Incarnation as enabling every one of us to become manifestations of Christ's salvific presence to others. Christ is born in us and grows in us (mostly through our experiences of suffering and limitation) to extend God's compassionate regard to the world.

> The mystery of Christmas therefore lays upon us all a debt and obligation to the rest of humanity and to the whole created universe. We who have seen the light of Christ are obliged, by the greatness of the grace that has been given us, to make known the presence of the Savior to the ends of the earth. This we will do not only by preaching the glad tidings of his coming, but above all by revealing him in our lives. Christ is born to us today, in order that he may appear to the whole world through us. This one day is the day of his birth, but every day of our mortal lives must be his manifestation, his divine epiphany, in the world which he has created and redeemed.

Puer natus est pro nobis—A Child is born for us yesterday, today, and forever!

Merton's Voice

From *Seasons of Celebration*

Christ is born. He is born *to us*. And, he is born *today*. For Christmas is not merely a day like every other day. It is a day made holy and special by a sacred mystery. It is not merely another day in the weary round of time. Today, eternity enters into time, and time, sanctified, is caught up into eternity. Today, Christ, the Eternal Word of the Father, who was in the beginning with the Father, in whom all things were made, by whom all things consist, enters into the world which he created in order to reclaim souls who have lost their identity. Therefore, the Church exults as the angels come down to announce not merely an old thing that happened long ago, but a new thing that happens today. For, today, God the Father makes all things new, in his Divine Son, our Redeemer, according to his words: *Ecce nova facio omnia. . . .*

At Christmas, more than ever, it is fitting to remember that we have no other light but Christ, who is born to us today. Let us reflect that he came down from heaven to be our light, and our life. He came, as he himself assures us, to be our way, by which we may return to the Father. Christ gives us light today to know him, in the Father and ourselves in him, so that thus knowing and possessing Christ, we may have life everlasting with him in the Father. . . .

Having realized, once again, who it is that comes to us, and having remembered that he alone is our light, let us open our eyes to the rising Sun, let us hasten to receive him and let us come together to celebrate the great mystery of charity which is the sacrament of our salvation and of our union in Christ. Let us receive Christ that we may in all truth be "light in the Lord" and that Christ may shine not only *to* us, but *through* us, and that we may all burn together in the sweet light of his presence in the world: I mean his presence in us, for we are his Body and his Holy Church. . . .

Christ, light of light, is born today, and since he is born to us, he is born in us as light and therefore we who believe are born today to new light. That is to say, our souls are born to new life and new grace by receiving him who is the Truth. For Christ, invisible in his own nature, has become visible in our nature. What else can this mean, except that first he has become visible as man and second he has become visible in his Church? He wills to be visible in us, to live in us, and save us through his secret action in our own hearts and the hearts of our neighbors. So, we must receive the light of the newborn Savior by faith, in order to manifest it by our witness in common praise and by the works of our charity towards one another. (pp. 102–105)

Another Voice

Christopher Bamford, *An Endless Trace: The Passionate Pursuit of Wisdom in the West*

The New Song: The Christian Mystery

It is the darkest night of the year, the dead of winter. Cut off from the sun's light, Earth has breathed in her soul. She lies silent and closed. Human beings, left to their own resources, are at their lowest ebb. Tempted by matter, deprived of the gods, they yearn for warmth and consolation. Then, suddenly, the New Creation breaks forth and the Sun of Righteousness rises, sounding in the ears of the universe, once and for always.

Light returns, the air grows warm with love. The days grow longer. The heavenly hosts, the angels of nations, the first to know, say to themselves (in Origen's words), "If he has put on mortal flesh, how can we remain doing nothing? Come, angels, let us descend from heaven." They come down to the shepherds and, praising God, announce the coming of the true Shepherd. On Earth, too, in the stable, all creation rejoices in the moment of redemption, the turn so long awaited and so ardently desired.

"Behold the night of the new song!" cries Clement of Alexandria. "It has made human beings out of stones, human beings out of beasts. Those, moreover, that were as dead, not being partakers of the true life, have come to life again, simply by listening to this Song." For Clement, the ineffable virtue of the Incarnation is that it is the universal medicine and elixir of life. By its healing power, matter and spirit are one. For all things first sounded into form in the Word; and now the Word, that melodious, holy instrument of God, made flesh in time, sounds out again, recalling all things to their wholeness and their home ground. . . .

Truly, in the history of the universe, regarded as the meaningful speech of human beings and gods, the Incarnation of God's Word marks the turning point. Speech having become flesh, flesh can become speech. Full, living meaning is restored. What God spoke outside time—in eternity—is now spoken, lives, and may be heard in time. No wonder that human beings who felt so destitute can suddenly feel joy and certitude. Clement's emotion is not hard to understand. The savior of creation, the creator, has come. The king of the world, the teacher of humanity—God's Word—has given himself. The cause of being has become the cause of well-being. The supernatural, having become natural, can become supernatural once more and God, according to the primordial desire never deviated from, can become all in all. This is the meaning of resurrection, the meaning of meaning. What a task for human beings! What a prospect! God has spoken and it is for humanity to listen and respond, to hear God's word and return God's speech.

Yet the Word is always with us—even to the end of the world—continuously begotten in an everlasting begetting, as brightness is begotten of light. As the life and truth in all things, this New Song warms and lights creation through a continuous act of love. To know this is to come to inhabit the limitless field of creativity outside time and nature but ever forming and creating it. It is to die to oneself and to find one's true other, one's true place and origin in the cause, essence, and source of all. It is to meet the bridegroom secretly and dwell in Paradise by the Tree of Life planted in every soul.

Realizing this, Eugen Rosenstock-Huessy wrote, "A Christian is a person to whom Christ speaks. The body of Christ is those who listen to him." More than that—through us, through cognition and consciousness, everyone and everything can and must listen, for all of creation groaned and travailed in pain for this, and all speech, like all love, is a single unity. Therefore, Rosenstock-Huessy continues, "As speakers as well as lovers, we need assurance that we move in a continuum, that our discovery of real life and our words make sense for ever and ever. Otherwise we go mad and all spirit leaves us. It is impossible to assume that when we speak we do something different from the peoples of all times. Our speech would be up in the air, a meaningless stammering, unless we have the right to believe that all speech is legitimate and authorized as one and the same life process from the first day on which man has spoken to the last" [see E. Rosenstock-Huessy, *The Fruit of Lips or Why Four Gospels* (1978) and *Speech and Reality* (1970)].

It is this tradition of those who listen before they speak that we must try to recover and make our own. The Word was spoken in the beginning and made all things; then, at the turning point of time, the Word was made flesh and dwelt among us. Now it is our turn. At the turn of the ages, when Christendom has all but disappeared and Christian teaching has practically been forgotten, we must connect with this tradition and set down for our time and way whatever we can find to know and tell. (pp. 87–89)

Reflect and Dialogue

What images, words, or sentences in these readings most resonate with your experiences? In what ways do they resonate?

How would you tell your children the meaning of Christmas?

How do you understand Eugen Rosenstock-Huessy's assertion that "A Christian is a person to whom Christ speaks. The body of Christ is those who listen to him"?

Has this practice of "contemplative dialogue" made a difference in how you have experienced Advent and Christmas in your life this year?

Closing

Conclude with one of the meditations on pages 57–58 or with a period of quiet reflection.

Closing Meditations

A.

My soul glorifies the Lord and my spirit rejoices
in God my Savior.
He looks on his servant in her nothingness.
Henceforth all ages will call me blessed.
The almighty does marvels for me.
Holy is his name.
His mercy is from age to age for those who fear
him.
He puts forth his arm in strength and scatters
the proud-hearted.
He casts the mighty from their thrones and
raises the lowly.
He fills the starving with good things and the
rich he sends away empty.
He protects Israel his servant, remembering his
mercy,
The mercy promised to our Fathers and to
Abraham and his sons forever.

Joseph Gelineau, translator

B.

The mystery of Christmas therefore lays upon us all a debt and obligation to the rest of humanity and to the whole created universe. We who have seen the light of Christ are obliged, by the greatness of the grace that has been given us, to make known the presence of the Savior to the ends of the earth. This we will do not only by preaching the glad tidings of his coming, but above all by revealing him in our lives. Christ is born to us today, in order that he may appear to the whole world through us. This one day is the day of his birth, but every day of our mortal lives must be his manifestation, his divine Epiphany, in the world that he has created and redeemed.

Thomas Merton
Seasons of Celebration, p. 112

C.

Too long have we assumed that it was enough to make up our minds and give intellectual assent to authoritatively declared truths, and that this was the whole of faith. Christian faith is not just a habit by which we are inclined to give assent to certain dogmatic information; it is a conversion of our whole being, a surrender of the entire person to Christ in his Church. It is an act of penance, the most fundamental act of penance, the *metanoia* [conversion] and entire change of heart which leads to the abandonment of our old understanding of our selves, of our relation to God and to the world, and to the discovery of our new identity in Christ.

Thomas Merton
"The Good News of the Nativity"
in *Love and Living*, p. 231

Sources

The Psalm texts in this work are from *The Psalms: An Inclusive Language Version Based on the Grail Translation from the Hebrew*. Published through exclusive license agreement by G.I.A. Publications, Inc. Copyright © 1963, 1986 by The Grail (England).

From Thomas Merton

Contemplative Prayer. Introduction by Thich Nhat Hanh. New York: Doubleday: 1996. Originally published as *The Climate of Monastic Prayer*. Cistercian Publications, 1969.

Love and Living. Naomi Burton Stone and Brother Patrick Hart, eds. New York: Harcourt, Inc., 1979.

Raids on the Unspeakable. New York: New Directions, 1964.

Run to the Mountain: The Journals of Thomas Merton, Volume One 1939–1941. Brother Patrick Hart, ed. San Francisco: HarperSanFrancisco, 1996.

Seasons of Celebration. New York: Farrar, Straus & Giroux, 1965.

Seeds of Destruction. Trappist, KY: Abbey of Gethsemani, 1964.

Another Voice

Bamford, Christopher. *An Endless Trace: The Passionate Pursuit of Wisdom in the West*. New Paltz, NY: Codhill Press, Inc., 2003.

Casey, Michael, O.C.S.O. *Strangers to the City: Reflections on the Beliefs and Values of the Rule of Saint Benedict*. Brewster, MA: Paraclete Press, 2005.

Clément, Olivier. *On Human Being: A Spiritual Anthropology*. Jeremy Hummerstone, trans. New York: New City Press, 2000.

LeClaire, Anne D. *Listening Below the Noise: The Transformative Power of Silence*. New York: Harper, 2009.

Straub, Gerard Thomas. "Falling Silent." © 2010 by Gerard Thomas Straub.

another voice

BIOGRAPHICAL SKETCHES

Christopher Bamford is the editor-in-chief of SteinerBooks and Lindisfarne Books. A Fellow of the Lindisfarne Association, he has lectured, taught, and written widely on Western spiritual and esoteric traditions, and is a contributing editor to *Lapis* magazine. He is the author, translator, and editor of numerous books, including *The Voice of the Eagle, Celtic Christianity, Ecology and Holiness, Homage to Pythagoras, Rediscovering Sacred Science,* and *The Noble Traveler.*

Michael Casey, O.C.S.O., is a Cistercian monk of Tarrawarra Abbey in Australia. He is the author of many books, including *Toward God,* a major and beautiful exposition of the spirituality of St. Bernard of Clairvaux, and *Fully Human, Fully Divine: An Interactive Christology.* He is among the finest Cistercian writers of our day.

Olivier Clément (1921–2009) was a French Orthodox theologian who was a member of the faculty of the St. Sergius Institute in Paris. He edited the theological journal *Contacts.* His book *The Roots of Christian Mysticism* is internationally recognized as a classic. Two other remarkable books of his have also been published in English: *Three Prayers* and *On Human Being: A Spiritual Anthropology.*

Anne D. LeClaire is the author of eight novels, including the critically acclaimed *Entering Normal* and *The Lavender Hour,* and her work has been published in twenty-four countries. She is a former reporter, radio news broadcaster and newspaper columnist. She lives on Cape Cod, Massachusetts. Visit her website at www.anneleclaire.com.

Joseph Gelineau (1920–2008) was a French Catholic Jesuit priest and composer, mainly of modern Christian liturgical music. Heavily influenced by Gregorian chant, he developed his Gelineau psalmody, which is used worldwide. Later he composed numerous chants for the ecumenical French Taizé Community.

Gerard Thomas Straub is the founder and president of the San Domiano Foundation, whose mission is "to place the power of film at the service of the poor." He has filmed and produced eleven films on world poverty and is the author of *The Sun and Moon Over Assisi*, *When Did I See You Hungry?*, *Thoughts of A Blind Beggar*, and *Hidden in the Rubble: A Haitian Pilgrimage to Compassion and Resurrection*.

The Merton Institute for Contemplative Living is an independent, non-profit organization whose mission and purpose is to awaken interest in contemplative living through the works of Thomas Merton and others, thereby promoting Merton's vision for a just, peaceful, and sustainable world.

Robert G. Toth served as the executive director of the Merton Institute for Contemplative Living from 1998 to 2009. He currently serves the institute as director of special initiatives.

Jonathan Montaldo has served as the associate director of the Merton Institute for Contemplative Living, director of the Thomas Merton Center, and president of the International Thomas Merton Society. He has edited or co-edited nine volumes of Merton's writing including *The Intimate Merton, Dialogues with Silence,* and *A Year with Thomas Merton*. He presents retreats internationally based on Merton's witness to contemplative living.